I0800840

Nature Theater of Oklahoma's

LIFE AND TIMES

Episode 2

53rd State Press
Brooklyn, New York

53SP 15
July 2013

ISBN no. 978-0-9857577-5-5
Library of Congress Control no. 2012955928

53rdstatepress.org

All characters and events – even those based on real people – are entirely fictional. Any resemblance to actual persons, living or dead, is purely coincidental.

LIFE AND TIMES

Episode 2

Conceived by PAVOL LISKA and KELLY COPPER
From a telephone conversation with KRISTIN WORRALL

Act 1.1

ROB

Hello! Hello…

How are you?

Heh!
Uhmmm.
So yesss!
So shall we continue?

Yes. Um. Yeah,
I think we were…
Around third grade,
Annnd.

Mr. Daccioli…
And Mr. Daccioli
And Cindy Legrand,
Who – Yeah, she was my
Best friend.
Annnd. Um… Hanging out with Mrs. Legrand
Like let's see.

But Mr. Daccioli, yeah.
He was a really tall Italian guy –
With sort of like –

Brownish orangish curly hair.
And he wore like – shaded glasses.
And he always wore a suit every day.
And um. He was

Like – reeeally like –
Always in a good mood, and he was –
Always encouraging us.
And it was the first time that like –

He would address all of the little kids –
In like a really adult fashion?
Like I was so used to adults
Speaking to me like a, you know, like a little kid.

So I really really liked him, and um.
He just – he encouraged us all to like –
Sort of take responsibility for ourselves.

Like I remember he uh,
He had some sort of system.

Oh shoot!
I don't exactly remember why –
Why it was.
But he had like a system.

Of like colors.
And.
If you acted like a baby or something –
I guess this is sort of like a baby thing anyway,
But he –
You know what?
Nevermind.
'Cause I don't remember it exactly,
But.

Act 1.2

ROB

I'll tell you about the time that um –
We won the creative writing contest,
And Um.
He took us all out. It was like –
He took the four winners of the month or something.
I'm not –
The highest winners or something.

And he took us out to… um.
Play miniature golf.
And. We went to a pizza parlor.
And. It was like by the sea.
And. One of the little kids – like got lost or something,
And there was this big –
And it was really like stressful!?
And I was really bummed.

Because it was this miniature golf outing
And I was so excited about –
And then it turned into like searching for the little kid.
And we ended up finding him.
And I don't remember where he went.

Act 1.3

ROB

But anyway, um.
See here.
Um. Alright.
Third grade.
Annnd. Uhhhhm.

I spent a lot of time with Cindy Legrand,
And I slept over at her house a lot.
And. I think I was telling you –
I hung out with her mother a lot.

And her mother was very Like –
She was one of those ladies who would be like:

ALISON

"I was soooo beautiful when I was young,
And I could have been a scientist,
But I got married instead."

ROB

And so she placed all of her hopes and dreams on Cindy.
And Cindy would get really mad.
Like she'd have these temper tantrums,
And then she'd like run off,
And so I'd be stuck
With Mrs. Le –
Ha ha!
Mrs. Legrand… heh!
Who I actually really liked!
And then we would just hang out all day.
And um.

Act 1.4

ANNE

Yeah, Cindy and I
Would play like dolls all day.
She lived in this –
Kind of like a house like mine,
But maybe a little smaller,
And like a little cozier.
And she had this room that was
All powder blue!
And she had a canopy bed
Which I wanted so badly,
But my mother didn't let me get one,
'Cause she thought they were gaudy.

ALL GIRLS

And she had sooo many dolls!
Like I had maybe like five dolls or something,
But I wasn't really attached to them;
But Cindy's dolls I loved.
And we would play with them all day, like –
Intricate like –
Looong epic!
Stories of you know.
It would be like:
"To be continued…"
"Next day…"
And um.

ANNE

And then!
The – the dolls were always of the domistic –

Domestic style, like mommy, child…
And then we would play like Barbie dolls once in a while.
And whenever we'd play with the Barbie dolls –
Then it would be like suddenly like –

ALL GIRLS They're all grown up, and like –
Everyone had like boyfriends!
And we would always like -- Ha heh!
Which was – and the – they –
Having them make out with –
With one another!

We were obsessed with like doing this –
Like you know, taking the two dolls and like –
Turning them so they – it's like they were kissing.
Annnd. Um.
That was very fun, but um.

Act 1.5

ANNE

And Actually!
(Oh God, I – this is – I –
Don't know if I should tell this story!
It's a little embarrassing…
But! Hhhah!
I guess I will!)

(big breath)

Cindy and I used to…
(Oh my God! It's gonna sound like all pervy, but) Mrrha ha!
We used to take baths together!
You know.
Just us.
Like you know…
As little children do!
And. Um.
Weeeee….
(Oh my God! I don't think I can tell this story!
It's reallly embarrassing!)
So. Maybe I'll skip –
Well – now that I'm – mhm.
Alright. Well –

ALL GIRLS

We used to play like –
As I said we were like obsessed with like –
The kissing, you know…

Oh! And another thing I used to do
With Mrs. Legrand all the time –
Is watch soap operas.
And that's how I like – started to become –
A big fan.
Of General Hospital.
And that's, you know, in third grade.
And – Cindy and I were both –
Really intrigued!
By the soap opera kiss.

ANNE You know we'd always ask her mother like –
"Why do they kiss that way?
It's sooo weird like – Why don't –?"
And Cindy would want to kiss her mother like that!
And her mother was like:
"No! You don't kiss ME like that!
That's just like – romantic kiss!"

(exhale)

And we were like completely perplexed!
And we wanted to – you know –
Kiss like that, because

ALL GIRLS It looked SO interesting! So.

ANNE So one time –
And in the bath Tub
We used to like – you know –

Play games or whatever.
And so then we were like –
"Let's do the soap opera kiss!"

So we used to go into the bathtub
And you know basically
Make out with one another!
And ha ha ha!
And then like –
You know, her mother
Would come in sometimes, and then –
One time her mother like came in, and –
We were making out;
And she's like – "Noo no!"

ALL GIRLS So! But she wasn't like at all like:
"What are you doing!?"You know.
'Cause we were little kids, so.
And she understood that we were fascinated by the –
Soap Opera Kiss.

So. So then we were like –
"Oh...
We can't really do that
With one another."
And. So then
Her mother was like –
"Oh yeah! You do that with boys!"
You know.

Act 1.6

ROB

And so.
This was also the time when Cindy became like –
She became like –
"Boy Crazy!"
As her mother – called it.

ALL GIRLS

And I –
I was definitely like – Boy Crazy,
But I was so shy! You know.
So I would never ever like –
Let on if I liked somebody.

ROB

And I think at around this time, too,
My mother was going to school.
Part time.
A lot.
Sooo, um.
I would come home –
From school,
And usually go right over to Cheryl or Cindy's house.
And uh.
And then.

Also, like just a huge memory
Of me being little is my father –
(I think I was saying this before, too, but)
Like coming home – I would
Come home from like Cheryl or Cindy's house and then

My mother – would be making dinner,
And my father would just like go down – stairs in the basement, and like –
Work in his like workshop or something, and
And I would always just like – there – we had this um –

ALL — Couch.

ROB — In our – kitchen.
And it had wooden –

ALL — Um.

ROB — Sides to it like – wooden – um.
What do you call it? –

ALL — Beams or something.

ROB — And I used to stare through the beams at my mother's–
And I remember –
At my mother while she was like

ALL — Making dinner.

ROB — And I remember, one time, thinking –
Like I was staring at her, while I was holding on to the beams,
And I was like –
"I have to remember this moment for the rest of my life!"

And I have another moment like that, too, like –
(Maybe a few years later, but.) Um.
And I was like staring at the – rug in the kitchen.
And the cabinets.
And Um
And then I – told my mother I was –
And she's like –
"What's wrong Bobby?"
And I was like:
"I have that feeling… like something's missing."

And. Um.
She's like:
"Something's missing? What do you mean?
Like – what – did you lose your ball or something?"

And I was like:
"No-nu-nu-no, I just like –"
So, I think it was like

ALL My first Existential Moment that I had.

ROB Uh heh hm.
Um. And I would always call it like
"The Feeling That Something's Missing"
And, um.
So, anyway.
Um. That was third grade.

Act 1.7

JULIE

Annnd. Um.
Oh, during the summer –
During the summertime,
We used to go um – up to New Hampshire.
And we would rent a condo.
For like two weeks.
In Waterville Estates.

ALL

And um. And I LOVED to go there, because
It was just like –
You'd go – to the pool.

JULIE

Annd um. There was like this huge –
It was just like a huge like – resort town?

But it wasn't very like resort-y.
It was really chill.
'Cause it was normally like a ski town, so –
During the summer it was not a lot of people…
And and uh –
they had like a lake.

ALL

And you would go to the lake and
You could rent a paddle boat,

JULIE

and – My brother and sister – and I would
Play like – SPY!

And we would – we would always like –
Pretend that we were like
spying on the other people
Like at the –
Like if there were a couple lounging on the beach or something We'd Like make up a story.

ALL — About them –
And it was always like –

JULIE — It was –
I think because I was really into soap operas.
I was really into like this idea
Of people having affairs all the time.
Like just the –

ALL — Everyone was having an affair!

ROB, JULIE, ANNE — And I always thought
My father was having an affair, you know. Ahem.
And also
My father…
Got Playboy Magazine.
And I was like:
"Oh my god!"
Like – And.

My mother would always like joke with my father like –
"Oh, you like – "
Oh and there was this lady –
There was this lady named Lorraine…

That he worked with.
And she'd always be:
"How's Lorraine?! How's Lorraine?"

And I was like:
"Oh my god my father's having an affair!"
But – but really I knew my father
Would never have an affair, because he's just like –
Just – Heh heh!
He –
It's just like – not in him.

ROB — But – I always like kind of GAVE myself that fantasy.

ALL GIRLS — Fantasy!

ROB — And I think my mother sort of did it to like

ROB, ANNE, JULIE — Spice things up!
I assume, between the two of them.

ALL GIRLS — *(Whispered)* Spice, spice, spice…

ROB — Um. And.
Oh and also! And I have to say that my –

ALL — Parents – would always be like –
Kissing one another.
They're always like – you know.
My mother – Especially my mother!
Would always be like kissing my m—father, and –

And they're very
affectionate towards each other, and –

ROB

And my father like –
You know, he's definitely…

I – I feel badly for my mother,
In a sense, that he is not –
Um. A communicator.
And sh—
I could see her get frustrated with him sometimes.

Like – sometimes we'd be – hm.
Sitting at the table, and she'd be like –"So!" –
She'd be like – mock like conversation.
She'd be like:
"So, Linda! How's your day going? Blah blah blah?"
You know, like be like –
"Come on, Bill! say something!"

Heh! You know.
But she would still kinda do it in like a –
Jovial way.
But I still was like:
"Oh, poor mom,"
You know. Um.

But – but he was always like do—
Always like making her stuff.

	And he would – On the weekends. Like every single weekend, he we would always make like – Breakfast for everybody. And it was like always like his food was like gourmet! Whereas my mother is a very good cook, you know. And she – like – now that I look back, she like – Busted her ass like – Making like really good meals for us. Every me – every night, but.
ALL	Whenever my father cooked it would be like: "Veal cutlet!" And he would spend like – heh! Like half an hour! Like tenderizing the meat. And you couldn't get – near him. Heh! Like he'd be like: "I'm in the kitchen!" As if it was like – This Grand Procession that was going on,
ROB	But. Um.

Act 1.8

ROB — So he would make her like fancy drinks…

ALL GIRLS — Fancy drinks!

ROB — At at night,
And – and –
He'd always — he'd call her "Baby".

ALL GIRLS — Baby!

ROB — Which I really loved –
Like when he called her Baby.
'Cause it was like –
"Oh!" It was really romantic.

ALL GIRLS — Romance!

ROB — Annd. Um. Hm.
And he – and during like Valentines Day?

ALL GIRLS — Valentines!

ROB — He would always like –
Give her these cards, and they –

ALL — He signed them sort of racily…
I don't remember, but he would say something like –

ROB — It was very like –
"I'm dying for you…!"
Or something.

ALL And I was like
"Ah! That's so nice!" –

ROB 'Cause I…
So I knew my father like –
Definitely like –

ALL Had a pulse!

ROB Eh heh hem!
'Cause otherwise…
I was like – "what –?"

ALL "What is going on with him?!"

ROB But, yeah.
The whole like Playboy Magazine, too,
Was like a little –
Like I was intrigued by it.
And whenever friends would come over, we would like –
Look through the Playboy Magazines.

ALL And he would st— he would store them –
In – the attic, too.
And, actually, um.
Yeah, I think… Heh!

ROB I think – they had to like
Hide it from my brother or something.

ALL 'Cause he probably would look through them, too.

ROB But um.
Anyway!
How did I get on the subject of Playboy Magazine?

ANNE I don't remember!

JULIE Um. My father....

Oh! We would go up to Waterville Estates!
Right! During the summer...
Oh, and yeah –

JULIE I was always thinking everyone had affairs.
And um. So, yeah.
Waterville Estates was really fun.
And, yeah, we would just do that.
That's really all I remember of our summers.
Like – otherwise summertime was just like –
Playing at other people's houses.

I think later on I started to go to camp,
But that's – A little later on,
When I was a little older,
But –
Ahem.
Um.

Act 1.9

ANNE

So. Hm. Um.
So, I guess let's turn to fourth grade!
Um.

Oh! And also,
At the time, too, um.
Oh, I have to tell you –
In third grade this girl –
Moved to Our town.
And her name was Lea Nieves.
She moved in the middle of the year.

And she was tiny.
She was a tiny little girl.
And she was like a year younger.
Um – than us.
But she skipped a grade or something.
And I – I became friends with her!

ANNE, ROB, JULIE, ALISON

But not – like very good friends, 'cause she –
Like everybody was friends with Lea, but –
She definitely really liked me, so.
I would go over her house once in a while,

ANNE

And she was the first friend –
I had
Whose parents were divorced.
And. Um.

And her mother… also had like –
A Rhode Island accent.
And um.

And she had –
She was really young.
Like compared to the rest of – hm – my friends' parents.
And her father also had a very bad
Rhode Island accent.
And He—

ANNE, ROB, JULIE, ALISON

He lived in Warwick – and we –
We would like hang out with him. Um.
Once in a while.
And he had a – big moustache.
And he was really nice. And he would always like –

ALL

Take us to Kaybee Toys!
And buy us – Um –
Puffy stickers.

But um. Anyway. It was really really fun to—to—
Hang out at Lea's house, because nobody was ever home.

And – and – we would –
I don't know. We just would play…
Really… um. Really fun games, and She had a pool.
And she – but she seemed – she seemed like –

Oh! And she had a water bed, too but and, oh!
And she had a stepfather, who was really big and burly, and –
And he – he got –
PENTHOUSE Magazine! And –
We would look through those, too.

ANNE

Oh and also, I had this friend, named Valerie Wilson.
And she was like the poorest girl, in the town.
And sh—her father owned um.
Or he was like a manager
at D'Angelos,
Which was like a submarine shop.
Ahem.
You know, like a sandwich shop.
And um.
And I remember one time – She had a like a little baby sister.
And I remember I was over there once–
and – the mother was like "Oh, no, like –
We can't finish that jar –
That, um carton of milk,
because –
We have to save it 'cause we – you know
We're on a – on budget for this week, for –
And we can't dip into next week's budget."
And I was like
Totally shocked
By that.

And I remember Valerie wanted to be a stripper
Heh! Or she was like –
And she was in third grade!
And she was like:

ALL

"I either wanna be a stripper
Or a Playboy model!" And – heh!
And she would always wear these like
REALLY see-thru Clothes!
And she had like – really really PALE skin,
and she had like Just really see-thru skin.
And she – I think she moved after like a year or so,
but. Anyway, she was like another
one of my mo—
Like – scandalous friends.
But um. Anyway.
(Oh my gosh, I'm totally jumping all around!)
But, anyway so okay. So fourth grade…

Act 1.10

JULIE I had a teacher – um.
Mrs. Steinberg,
And The classroom we had was like
Longer. And –
After third grade,
I remember it was like suddenly –
I think it, yeah.
Because we were entering more like

ALL Adolescent – years.
We all felt like a little more – grown up,
And I think –

JULIE Like people started having like –
Boyfriends and girlfriends.
Like beyond just like:
"Oh, you – I like him! You like me!"
It was like – people established like:

ALL "Oh, I'm going out with Blah blah blah…"

JULIE And um. Annnd…
In fourth grade –
I don't really remember much about that year,
But –I was a really good student.
And I was like –

ALL	And everyone like sort of acknowledged That I was like the smartest kid in the class, And I – really wanted to maintain that status.
JULIE	And um. Heh heh. And uh! I don't really remember much from fourth grade.
ALISON	Except – Um. One time – we had like a party!
ALL	And. Um. We made like cupcake – Like everyone made cupcakes Or like Rice Krispie squares… And it was like: "Yay! Fun!" And. Um. And I just remember like dancing around to… Um – that song: "The – Angel is a centerfold!" And. And while we were dancing around – Um my friend Cheryl was like – Behind this kid, Michael Ellston.
ALISON	And she like bumped him by mistake. And – he got really mad at her… And they got in like a physical fight.
ALL	And then she kicked him – Like IN THE BALLS! (Like I hate using that word, but…)

He – she did.
And so it was like HUGE scandal,
And like she was sent home.
And. Um.

ALISON — And she – I think she was like suspended.

ALL — For like a week or something.
And. And my mother – was like:
"Oh… really? She –?"
And so, she you know
Didn't really encourage me
To hang out with her that much.
So.

Act 1.11

JULIE — Cheryl and I – for the next like year, actually…
I think we sort of got in a big fight.
I think it was that year.
And she used to send me notes
Like: "Can U B my friend?"

ALL — And I – I didn't wanna become her friend.
Because at this time she was like –

JULIE — After the whole like kicking Michael Ellston…
She became like sort of the social pariah.
And – I didn't want –
To link myself to her.
Sooo. Um.

And I was also increasingly more –
Like I, you know – as I said

ALL — I was – I really wanted to be the first –
The smartest person in the class.
But. And. And.
And I really wanted to be popular.
And um.

JULIE — Ahem.

So…And also Cheryl – Cheryl her –
Father, since he was a pilot,
He would Go to Japan a lot –

And he would get her … these um –
Designer clothes… like fake designer clothes.
And they looked so fake,
And she was just an awful dresser.

ALL — And I was really concerned with how I looked,
And I was always just like:
"Oh god, she's just SO TACKY!"
So. I COULDN'T become friends with her!

JULIE — And I didn't feel badly about it.
And uh.

She would send me notes,
I remember. And. And –
I remember – ha ha ha!
I remember one note –
She sent me, she was like:
"What kind of music do you think my mother listens to?

And I was like – Ahhhheh!
And I wrote back:

ALL — "Your mother listens
to really gay music!"
Um. "It's really –" Heh! "Slow and boring!"

JULIE — And – And then she wrote back:
"No, she doesn't! She listens to soft rock!"

And I was like:
"Oh, ri— whatever!"
Ha!

ALL OH MY GOD!

Anyway. Yeah.
I don't really remember much from fourth grade.

Act 1.12

ANNE

But I became like increasingly more like awkward, too.
Like – looking.
Or at least like I felt like I did.
And I was like kinda lanky…
And I was um.
I was – I was tall for my age.
Definitely.
And um.
But I remember going to the doctor, and he was like:
"Oh, you're tall now,
But you're not gonna be tall later."

And I was really like mad.
Because my mother really –
Like whenever we would like meet somebody
Who was pretty or something…
Or like handsome. Like tall, I knew, was –
Always like a good thing.
And I was like: "Oh…"

(exhale)

And um.

Act 1.13

ANNE

And. I think also yes!
At this time um.
I wasn't like developed at all.

ALL GIRLS

But this other girl, Karen Oliver,
Had really big boobs.
And all of the boys liked her.

So. I think she was
Like the only person who –
Actually like – started developing, and so.

It wasn't like a huge like:
"Oh no! What's happening to me?"
Because nobody else was.
But uh we were all like
Starting to become aware.
And oh! And this is the time
When we all read um. The Book:
Are You There, God? It's Me, Margaret.

And um, I don't know if you know that book, but uh.
We were all read it like maybe five or six times.
And it was actually banned from um.
It was banned from our school library.

Because the boys would take it out all the time.
Because it talked about –
Periods and um
Developing boobs, but uh –
(They didn't call them "boobs"… like… I don't know: "breasts")

ANNE And. Um.
Ehrm.
So, all of us girls – would um.
Talk about getting our periods,
And there was this exercise
That we would do that was
Described in the book, which –
It wasn't really described closely,
But we sort of made up our own version of.

ALL GIRLS And we used to clasp our hands
Together like um.
As if you're squeezing something.
And put your arms out in a circle,
Before you.
And you just like – um.
Clasp your palms together and you go:
"I must! I must! Increase my bust!"

ANNE Heh!
And you just do it like – 50 times.
And um.

I think maybe in fifth…
No, probably sixth grade, I –
Yes!

So that's like – jumping around, so.
Nevermind.

Act 1.14

ALISON

Um. Soooo. Yeah,
And I think I cut bangs for the first time, too,
Because I was really self-conscious of --
My very long forehead.
And I used to… um.
I remember I used to look
In the mirror in my bathroom,
And there was like –
And my bathroom it was yellow. It was all yellow.
And. Um.

You know we had the sink and then the bathroom,
And I used to measure – my height.
By looking at my forehead.
So as I got older, all I would just see
Is this like huge forehead.
And just like my eyebrows.
And I was ju— Like:
"Oh my god!"

Act 1.15

ROB

Also, like just a huge memory
Of me being little is my father –
(I think I was saying this before, too, but)
Like coming home – I would
Come home from like Cheryl or Cindy's house and then

My mother – would be making dinner,
And my father would just like go down – stairs in the basement, and like –
Work in his like workshop or something, and
And I would always just like – there – we had this um –
Couch.
In our – kitchen.
And it had wooden – um.
Sides to it like – wooden – um.
What do you call it? –
Beams or something.

And I used to stare through the beams at my mother's –
And I remember –
At my mother while she was like
Making dinner.

And I remember one time thinking –
Like I was staring at her, while I was holding on to the beams,
And I was like –
"I have to remember this moment for the rest of my life!"

Act 1.16

JULIE And um.
So. What else?
What… else?
I don't know.
So.

ALL Then. Yeah, I guess,
Like fifth grade rolled around.
And. Yeah! Like I liked –
I really liked school.
But. Um.
I was Yeah.
Definitely…more con—
I was – as I got older –
Like more and more concerned with like:
"Oh no, I'm not like a popular kid."
And the popular kids were like

Johnna!

ELISABETH Johnna Mollicone.
I think still went to our school at this point.
And she was like a BIG snob.
And at this point.
And she – erhm.
Barely talked to anybody.
And she um.

ALL Johnna!

ELISABETH Johnna Mollicone, yeah.
This was the girl I was like best friends with
In kindergarten.
And she like never spoke to me,
You know, 'cause I didn't…
And she like always
Wore like Gloria Vanderbilt…jeans.
Which I bought –

ALL Oh, no, not Gloria – !
She used to wear like Calvin Klein!
Like the real ones!
And I always wanted to wear them,
But my mother would just –
Take me to TJ Max.
And I'd get like the rip offs.
I'd get – Like Gloria Vanderbilt I had.
And…And I loved those!

ELISABETH Those were like my first designer jeans,
And then I got – a pair of –
Ahem. Vidal Sassoon jeans,
But those were – really fake.
Vidal Sassoons. Or Sassoon jeans.
And uh.

I think I – I did get a pair of – Calvin Klein jeans.
But they were really fake looking.
So. Wasn't so into them.
And…

Act 1.17

ELISABETH

Everyone, too, was very concerned with their sneakers.
And um.
I was so happy when I got my first pair of Nikes.
They were white
With yellow… little swooshes.
Annnd uhm.
Anyway.

JULIE

Yeah, and, too, the other popular people were like:
Michelle Gossman.

And she was kind of like –
It's weird!
Because, you know,
I don't remember… like –

ALL

You know we're all like in fifth grade, for God sake!
But. Um. Everyone had –
Like the popular girls at the time
Like had this air
Of being like sluts
Or something.

But I'm sure they didn't do anything!
But like –
There was just this –
Like maybe they would talk about it, and – um.

Act 1.18

ANNE

At the time I was – you know – I was –
Absolutely frightened, of boys.
I mean I was like – you know.
I had big crushes on people,
But so the idea of like –
Even like having a conversation with one was –

You know, the only boy that I could talk to was like
Alan Silverman. Heh!
Who sat next to me, and he had orange hair.
And he had a really bad um,
Like allergy problem.

And he was always like –
Sniffing!
Ah heh heh!
And he was really smart.
And um.
He was actually –

Yeah. He was like probably, yeah.
The smartest person in our class.
I shouldn't say I was.
But, people like liked me more.

He was just like a big nerd, you know.
Like that's all he was – was smart.
Like he was:

"Yes! 16 times 52 is – blah blah blah blah"
You know.
So he was sort of like inhuman!

Um. But, so I could talk to Alan, or like –
Brett Hoff.
He was really annoying though.
He was another nerd, and then –
Uh – Yeah a couple of others.
Oh, and Brad Jackvony!
So I could talk to the nerds,
But like the cute boys I could not, and.

ROB

And, yes. At, I think –
I mentioned at the time, too,
Cindy Legrand –
My very good friend.
You know she always had…
Like – boyfriends.
And she – actually…
Her first
Like big boyfriend was um.
Joey Barbieri!
And I had such a crush –
On Joey Barbieri!
And I really thought
That he really liked me, too.
Ahem.

But it was all in my mind,
Because then he decided he liked Cindy,
And, I guess –
Like she showed me the note,
And it was like:
"Will you be my girlfriend? Check Yes or No."
And I was – I was like so crushed.

ALL GIRLS *(Whispered)* So crushed, so crushed…

ROB But I – of course – never told her that I
Ever liked him
Or anything.

Ahem.
And um.
They used to uh…
They used to like hold hands
During lunch.
And stuff.
And uh.

(exhale)

Act 1.19

ALISON

And also at the time,
During lunch time,
We – during recess we used to have um.
Boys Chase Girls Day

And maybe this is run – Yeah!
This is running into sixth grade, too, but um.

A very – traumatic –
Uh. Heh! Recess.
I remember once.
And it was like really violent –
But um.
For all of us.

But – we had um.
The Boys Chase Girls Day and suddenly –
You know, we would have this
Every once in a while.
But this one day, it suddenly became like
The boys would like –
Were taking the girls and they were like –

ALL GIRLS

Pulling our hair…

ALISON

They were –

ALL GIRLS

Taking our shoes, and they were like

ALISON — Putting dirt in it…
It was

ALL — Like LORD OF THE FLIES!
Kind of thing.

ALISON — It was – really –
And I – I remember like –

ALL — Running… for my life!
You know.

ALISON — Like I felt so…
Like absolutely like – frightened!

And, uh. There was like –
After that day… like
There were a few girls –
Who were like hurt and stuff.
And like – had to go to the nurse, and…
I – I think I escaped
Or something, but – heh!
And after that day we had like –
You know, some sort of um …session.
Like you can't like –
You have to be nice to one another.

Act 1.20

ROB — And I think we even, at this time, too…
(Uh, no…nununo. That was later on. But –)

It reminds me of in Junior High we had um –
You know how you have like –

ALL — Racial Awareness!

ROB — And. We had –

We were each assigned a color
And we had to like pretend
To have this like – caste system.
Where like orange, you're like a

ALL — Cool person, and –

ROB — And green per— like green people,
Had to like carry the orange people's books.

Anyway! It was like
One of those stupid things
That really didn't work at all,

ANNE — But. Um. Soooo. Yeah.
And then, so sixth grade
Though, definitely – that was like –
The year where I was like –
I decided…

Like in my brain.
I remember just being like:
"I can't wait 'til I'm adult.
I can't wait to get outta here."
Like I hated…
Not – I didn't hate… all the other kids,
But I just was like:
I des—
Like "Get me away…from these people!"
I just want to be an adult!
And I like – couldn't wait.
So.

JULIE | My friends and I –
Which were like, at this point, um –Oh!
Cheryl and I –
We made up!
Like I decided to be her friend again.
Because, um –
I don't remember why,
But I guess I really missed her, you know.
So.

In sixth grade…
Sheee and – um like – uh.
Maybe two other girls, we formed –

JULIE, ANNE | This like Secret Group.
And we all…um kind of –
And I still have – heh!

All the like – papers from it…
But we formed like our own like -- identities.

JULIE — And my name –
I don't remember my name! Sh—
It's like something like Violet? … Somebody…
Ha! And I was a fashion designer.

JULIE, ANNE — And I – on my – and –
You're supposed to write like a bio. Or something…
And I –
And I like lived in Italy.

JULIE — And. Um. I…
Yeah. Anyway!
Ha! Heh…
And I remember… hahahaha!
Oh my god! I'm…
Um. I – remember on the papers…

JULIE, ANNE — Like we had official papers of like our identity.

JULIE — And I wrote like the insignia for my jeans on the back.
It was like: "Violet Blahblahbla…" Anyway
And there's like a big flower.

JULIE, ANNE — Um so we used to play this game –
I don't remember what we would DO, but –
We would –

JULIE Take on – these personas,
And – we… would like stage –
MURDERS!

There was like some –
Like always we had to like –
Solve a murder or like a mystery or—
And we would always like –
Walk behind –
To like the other schools,
And – and uh…
We just would not socialize with any of the other kids,
And I was like:
"Ohmygod YES!

ALL Get me outahere!"

JULIE And it's very funny, because I look at –
My like class – picture
Heh! Of that year, and I'm like –
Scowling! Ha! Oh My GA!
I just was like kind of starting
To become really miserable.

(exhale)

And um.

Act 2.1

ANNE

And at this time, too, like –
I would go over Cheryl's house after school.
And wee – we were like:
"Oh let's start smoking!"
And so – we –

We didn't wanna go buy cigarettes '
'Cause like we were too young,
So, we would like –
We would take like tea bags…
And we would roll them…
In cigarette – things.

And we tried like – banana leaves…
And we tried like nutmeg,
And all these different things.
But they didn't really work.
And we would go to this like – um –
Weird tree pla— clearing.
And we would try to

ALL

Smoke them in the woods!

ANNE

And we would go –
On her rooftop a lot, too.
And we would sunbathe.
But um.

ROB — Oh God! Yes!…
(I'm remembering
Lots of things now!)
There was this boy –
Who moved to town,

And his name was Shon Campbell.
And he lived up the street from me,
In this really big house.
And um, his father like had like
A very successful like painting business.

And um. So anyway, Shon Campbell…
He like moved from like – Cranston or something –
Which is another town like a couple of towns away

ALL — And People who live in Cranston have like –
Really bad Rhode Island accent.

ROB — And he Had buck teeth, too.
And he was a break dancer!

ALL — And he wore like really flashy clothes!
And he was really into Van Halen.
And he'd always play – Van Halen.
And I actually – like –
When he would play I'd be like:
"Oh, that's really – good."

And oh! At the time…

ALL I was really starting to get into music.

ROB And that was like – Ah!

ALL That was another like reprieve from like –

ROB "Oh – my – God. I hate – my life."
Sort of thing.
And I was really in to The Police.
And I think –

Act 2.2

ROB	At first I was into The Police, because – My sister… was into them. And the – whatever my sister was into like – I was like –
ROB, JULIE, ANNE, ALISON	I thought my sister was like The Coolest Thing In The World. So like I would like – Try to dress like her… I would listen to whatever she listened to… And then I was like, you know, Maybe I should start listening to music. So. I would listen to her um – Police records. And I really really loved them.
ROB	And then – I started – to like – um. I started to like become Obsessed with them, actually. And I – I – I bought Like all these like Po—Police books.
ROB, JULIE, ANNE, ALISON	And I cut out – All the pictures of Sting. 'Cause I thought he was beautiful And I made this like – Big collage in my room Heh! And I –

ALL — And it was ALL STING!

ROB — And I remember one day my mother like walked in
And she was like –

ALISON — "Bobby… I just don't understand, like!
I was never LIKE that, as a little girl…
Like I never got…
I never…was like –
Into like movie stars, or anything…"

ROB — And I was like:
"Well I – AM!"
And – ha ha ha!
Ummm….
But I really, you know.
I would like stare at his pictures, and I thought, like –
You know.
He loved me too, sort of thing.
And I remember I had this book
and it was like:

ALL — "What are Sting's favorite foods?"
And – and HIS favorite foods was:
Steak and Baked potato and red wine.

ROB — And I was like:
"Oh I rea—! I wanna like that!"
But I really didn't like steak very much.
But. Um.
Anyway.

Um, but I really –
I did really begin to grow to –
Love the music a lot.
And there was this other boy in my class –
Danny Cohen.
Who – also really liked The Police, so!
I had like sort of – like a comrade.
As a boy –
Who – you know.
And I, you know,
Would talk to him about music.

Act 2.3

ROB

And I also really liked um –
I liked Genesis. A lot!
Um.
Who – at the time –
Like Phil Collins… was the lead singer.
And uh. I would listen to that song – um.
What was it called?
It was like – "If I…"
It was something about like –
"If I saw you drowning I wouldn't – I wouldn't –
Save you."
Or something.
What is that Song?
It's "Something in the Air Tonight"!
A—And anyway that song–
The whole song –

Is like very macabre, and it's about like –
And there's uh –this urban legend.
Attached to it –
That like – um.
One of – Phil Collins… friends…
Was drowning…
Uh – you know --
I don't know the story.
But anyway!

I – I was like really –
I was very drawn to all these like dark –
Things. You know?

Act 2.4

ROB And uh, And then.

Also, like just a huge memory
Of me being little is my father –
(I think I was saying this before, too, but)
Like coming home – I would
Come home from like Cheryl or Cindy's house and then

ALL My mother – would be making dinner,
And my father would just like go down – stairs in the basement, and like –
Work in his like workshop or something, and

ROB And I would always just like – there – we had this um –

ALL Couch.
In our – kitchen.
And it had wooden – um.
Sides to it like – wooden – um.
What do you call it? –
Beams or something.
And I used to stare through the beams at my mother's –
And I remember –
At my mother while she was like
Making dinner.

And I remember one time thinking –
Like I was staring at her, while I was holding on to the beams,

And I was like –
"I have to remember this moment for the rest of my life!"

JULIE And um.
Although I do remember!

Oh my god… ha ha ha!
I can't believe you're doing this!
This is good! Ha ha ha!
Oh my god! Oh my god!

Act 2.5

JULIE

I do remember the first movie I went to by myself.
At Showcase Cinemas!
And it was with Kathy D'Orio
And um, we went to go see Ghostbusters.
That was very fun.

And I also remember a –
Yeah! I remember seeing movies a lot.
And that was when Showcase Cinemas – was –
It was like right down the street, really.
And um, and –
We would go there a lot.

And, unfortunately – Oh my god! –
One time…
My mother was like:
"I'll take you and Cheryl to the movies!"
Annnd…
And I was like:
"Oh. Cool. That's great."

And so…
She took us –
(I don't remember what movie it was…)
But she took us, and then I was like:
"Well, we're gonna sit in the back!"

And she was like:

"But I wanna si—
I wan—
I took you guys—!
Like – I wanna – I wanted to take you guys…"
And I – feel – so badly now.
But – I was like:
"No!"

ALL "NO! NO! NO! NO! NO! NO! NO! NO! Nooooo!"

JULIE Like I –
This was the point, too of where –
You know –
I was so embarrassed to be seen with my mother.
Or my father.
And I started to become –
Kind of mean to my parents.
And I didn't really talk to them anymore.

And – and my mother
Was so hurt!
And she was like:
"Alright. Fine."
And she left.

But I didn't KNOW how to be like –
I didn't know how to say I'm sorry.
So I just – Like I felt
Really badly, but I was like:
"Euh!"

Like I Cared too much about –
About being alone with my friend at the movie theater.
And not being seen with my mother.

And uh.
And alllsssso…
(I – you…oh…)

Oh yeah! So we watched lots of movies.
My brother and me.
Um. And yes.
In sixth grade… was like –
Yeah, just like –
The Beginning of the Dark Period.

Act 2.6

ALISON

Yeah – I was – very.
I was becoming more and more very awkward,
And very like self-conscious.
And. So yes –
So by the time, yes –
Then Junior High like rolled around.

And I was like so excited to go to Junior High.
Because I was like:
"Oh, finally
I can feel like an adult…"

And…I could go to classes,
And like I had like Spanish class!
And you know we all have different schedules…
And it was just very exciting, you know.
And.

I – at this time, too –
I was very concerned…
As I was before, too…
But even more so now –
About my clothes.
And I would like –
I had this calendar…
Of like what I was gonna wear each day –
And – and at the time
This label – called Esprit –

Uh, it was sort of like – you know –
A girls clothing line…
Like was very popular.
And I used to count how many Esprit –
Pieces of Esprit clothing I have.

And at this time, too, my mother –
She had graduated from school,
And now she had a job,
So she had like extra money,
So like she would take me –

I think my mother really wanted to bond with me.
Because my sister –
Was very very like –
Bad kid, you know.
She just was like always like getting into trouble…

And so I think my mother viewed me as like:
"Oh… you know I really want to bond with her!'
And I was also like – much sweeter and nicer --
Heh! Of a kid – than my sister was.

So… my mother… would –
Take me to the mall like
Every weekend.
And she'd buy me all these clothes.
So I had – a really nice clothes.
And – for – you know – a little kid, at the time.
And so –

Even though I was very like awkward and everything –
This being Junior High…
Um.

And I – in Junior High, too,
You meet all these other new kids
From the other – elementary schools all come together.
So all these people…
Like had this like interest in me!
'Cause I dressed really well, you know.
And uh –
And I felt very uncomfortable
With that.
I was like – "Oh my god!"

Like I felt like – I had to somehow…
Keep up –
The appearance.
So I just felt – the pressure of like –
I had to be really cool,

And I didn't Feel…
I wasn't confident –
Enough, you know.

JULIE

And at the time, too, Cheryl…
I was friends with Cheryl.
And she (once again) – was like –
Heh! The social pariah, you know.
And…uh… so I was like –

I…
We had this –
Like – you –

Within the first
Couple of weeks –
Of Junior High –
We had this um – uh.
What do you call it –
Election!
For – The like –
Student Council Representative.
Of each homeroom.

And I remember they voted me IN!

And I was like –
I was like absolutely –
Like shocked!
You know
'Cause I, you know –
I – I didn't know any of these people.
And – and so then um.

I remember this girl –
Stacy Clemmens. Uhm.
(Was her last name Clemmens?
No! It couldn't have been…)
Stacy Wright!
Yes. Stacy Wright.

Who sat behind me in Junior High. Uh in –
Homeroom class.
She was like:
"D'you wanna sit with us at – at um…LUNCH?"
And I was like: "Okay!"
So I got to sit with like all the –
Like extremely popular,
Very Like you know –
Pretty, cheerleader-ish girls.

And I just felt – so uncomfortable.
And I didn't know what to say,
And then the next day I was like:
"You know what – ?
I'm just gonna be friends with Cheryl."

So I started becoming…
I like was like:
"I'm – friends with Cheryl."
And then from that time on –
Stacy Wright like never talked to me.
And uh…

In fact one time…
I remember we –
And we at the time, too,
In Junior High we had lockers!
And I was like at my locker.
And I was like putting my books back in.
And – and uh –

Stacy Wright was next to me, and –
At the locker –
And like some other girl
Like came over.
And she was like: "Oh!…Um…"
She asked me a question.
Or she tried to ask me a question or something.
And Stacy was ju— was like:
"Don't talk to her, she's a loser!"

(gasp)

And I was like: "Ooooh – Myyy – God!
I'm a FUCKING LOSER!"
Mrh heh haha ha!
You know, 'cause it was like –
The Losers…!? And then The Popular Girls!
You know, and then I was like:
"Oh my God!"
So, uhm. Sooo, yes.
So I felt – like: "Oh my god."
I was MISERABLE!
Heh heh!

I like –
And I sat behind –
Um, Matt Wolf… who I had the biggest crush on.
Um. He was very cute.
And he talked to me
A lot!

I think Stacy Wright was just mean, too,
She wasn't necessarily like the most popular girl.
She just didn't like me.
Because I like kind of –
You know, I – said I was going to be friends with her,
And then I didn't.
Heh.

I don't think REALLY in the span of it I was a big loser, but –
But – I think.
Yeah.
Um.
Stacy – she was just mean.

Act 2.7

ANNE

But. Um. Soooo. Yeah.
And then, so sixth grade
Though definitely that was like –
The year where I was like –
I decided…
Like in my brain.
I remember just being like:
"I can't wait 'til I'm adult.
I can't wait to get outta here."
Like I hated…
Not – I didn't hate… all the other kids,
But I just was like:
I des—
Like–"Get me away…from these people!"
I just want to be an adult!
And I like – couldn't wait.
So.

Act 2.8

ALISON	But. Um. Anyway Let's see… Yes, and then, um – I had band Class, too. Which was like Another Big thing.
ALL GIRLS	And Mr. Stabile was the conductor. And he was really Short guy, and um. He would sort of like flirt! With all – Like me, And and with Cindy Legrand…
ALISON	Um. Who was – you know, The clarinet player. And we were – Like – both like "First Chairs" you know. And he'd – I don't know!
ALL GIRLS	It was just like a weird flirtation. But we didn't like think it was strange at all… You know. But now – Heh! Like he's – I guess little strange!
ALISON	But um and then there were all the um – percussionists. That he would kind of like –

Um. Joke with. Too.
Because I think – also, too,
It was like –
The drummers in the band were really good.
And then –

Cindy and I were good musicians,
And so –
He like –
Talked to us like he –

ALL

We were like adults.
And the rest of the kids were like –
Just really bad or something!
So he didn't really… pay much mind to them,
But – the drummers… Um –
Like everybody loved them.
And there was – um.

ALISON

Michael Flynn.
Was was the um –
The –
One of the drummers, and –
He, I have to say, was like –
My – my first like –
I know I mentioned I had like about a billion
Crushes before, but – he was like

My first like –
Like heartcrushing

Like like – I would see him walking down the hall,
And I'd be like: "Blh…"
You know, my heart would just like –
Heh! Start like beating!

I just like thought –
He was so gorgeous!
He had brown hair,
And it was sort of like wavy…
And he had these like
Really small, but really like piercing eyes.
And he was just – so cute!!
He was so cute.
And he was really sweet.
He was probably a little… dumb, you know.

But he was in my Spanish Class, and I
Would just like stare at him the whole time.
And every time like –
I would like – you know –
Look another direction –
My eyes would still be like –

ALL FIXATED on Michael Flynn, you know.
I was – it was actually like a –

ALISON And um. So
And Cheryl, actually.
Also garnered a crush on him, too.

And we used to call him "G.G.!"
For like… um. Code Name.
And we just would
Write like notes all during class about:
"G.G… G.G…."

ELISABETH And um.
At seventh grade, too like –
Was the first time that um.
I was in… chemistry class was it?
And – I just didn't get chemistry at all! So…
It was the first time I was – I was like –
A pretty bad student.
I like – yeah.
I – and it –
If it weren't for my father like tutoring me every day in it,
I would of – probably like failed chemistry.
'Cause I just did NOT get it at ALL.

ROB And –
And I was also like –
My god…!
Cheryl and I would like write –
Notes to each other and we'd be like –
We were so depressed! All the time!
We'd just be li— "I wanna kill myself!
Oh my God! Get me out of here!"

Like we were just like the most depressed kids.
And it's really weird!
Because I don't know
What I had to be depressed about.
Other than like –
Just like – yeah.
Like adolescent malaise.
And um.

ALISON But Cheryl, I think she had a really bad…
Home life! And I probably took a lot of it on,
Like – at this point, too,
She'd like call me…
For like hours upon end.
And just like be crying
About her father and stuff.

ROB And – um. So… anyway…
Yeah, I was
Just like a depressed kid.

And I remember, too…
Um, I was a candidate
To be in the National Honors Society!
And um. I didn't make it in, because I
And I – I had a little meeting with my student councilor,
And she's like:

ALL "The reason why you didn't make it in, Bobby,
Is because you have a really Bad Attitude."

ROB — Heh ha ha!
And I was – like: "Oh my god!"

And I didn't think I did at all!
I was just –
I really thought I was just like –

I – I felt misunderstood.
And I felt like really – I was just
Really depressed Kid, you know.
And I was really

ALL — Kinda bummed out that like nobody…

JULIE — It was kind of like that day –
That I told my mother that she couldn't watch the movie with me.
I was like – kind of hoping
That she… would understand
That – I like –

I wasn't really being mean,
But I was like – I was so concerned with –
You know, how it looked.
And I – and I wanted her to –
Understand the subtext,
But she didn't. So I was –
And I was hoping all my teachers… would, too.
But – you know
They just saw me as a brat, you know.

But I was really just like:
"Oh my god!
I'm really a NICE KID!
But I just don't know how to uh – communicate it!"
You know.

So... Um. Yeah.
And then eighth grade,
I just became more and more – like
Awkward looking!
And my skin started to break out.

ALL

And... I had braces...
And I just was like an AWKWARD kid, you know!

JULIE

And I was just
Kind of miserable
And I would always just, you know.
Duck in the back.
Of class, and uh.
I had my few, like – girlfriends, but.

ALL

I – Junior High was very painful.

JULIE

Heh he he heh.
It was like – heh!
"I'm getting this over right now!"

And also like I had some teachers who...
Like I remember uh.
My social studies teacher from eighth grade...

I don't remember her name.
But she would like –
Play favorites
With everybody!
And she liked all the popular kids,
And I was just like –
"Ugh! My god!
Why does she like all the boring popular kids!?"

ALL Like – it's just the beginning of like Social Injustices!
You know.
And um. It was just like – yeah.
I just was like –
"This is – SHIT!"

JULIE You know.

Act 2.9

ROB

Yeah, uhm…
And I – you know, too, as I said –
At the time, too,
Like I never talked to my parents…

And – at this point –
And my father sometimes would –

Take me to school.
And he had a company car.
Which was like – this Ford
That was kind of like falling apart.
I don't know WHY they gave him this! Like –
Such a SHITTY car!
Heh! It was like – falling apart!
And I was like –
Always so embarrassed for him!
To drop me off, you know.
Just like –
"Jesus Christ!"

ALL

And now that I look back –
What a fucking waste of—
I was just so concerned
What other people thought about me.
And um. Soooo.

ROB

Yeah, and it –
And uhh…

ALL	I used to like make fun Of what my father was wearing… All the time! And he would like – try to like – you know – Bond with me.
ROB	And I just wouldn't have it, you know. And it's just too bad. But anyway, um.
ALISON	Also, at this time, too. I would go away with Cindy on vacations. We would go to like Florida. And that was really fun. 'Cause my parents never – Well, I mean we all went to New Hampshire all the time, But it was always like these very like – Wholesome sort of things. But we went to like Disneyworld with Cindy's family, And and uh. That was very fun. And we drank – Heh! Grape juice! Wheh! And stuff like that! Grape juice! And just like – You know stuff that I normally didn't eat or drink or anything. Anyway…

Ummm.
(Oh God…)
I just could tell you
Soooo many fucking stories!
It's just like –
But they're ALL so meaningless –

ROB I – okay, but there's also this one –
This One Story.
(Uh, not story…)
But this one time –
That I went away with Cindy.

W— She— I would go to Vermont with her a lot.
Um her parents –
Her mother had a sister
Who lived out there.

She lived on a farm.
And um.
Wee uhhhh…
We would stay in – she –
They always rented a camper!
And um.

That was always really fun, too.
My parents would never have rented a camper, you know.
They would never have rented a camper.

	So that was very fun for me to go in this camper, And we would sleep in the camper.
ALL	You know.
ROB	And um. They had a like a sauna…
ALL	*(Whispered)* Sauna!
ROB	Um. On – in the – On the outside.
ALL	*(Whispered)* Outside!
ROB	And. Um. I remember she had this cousin.
ALL	*(Whispered)* Cousin!
ROB	Who, uh. Who like – was older. And –
ALL	Cindy was like in love with him.
ROB	And um she was like –
ELISABETH	"Oh no! I can't like – can't love him Because he's my cousin!"

ROB — And I was –
Like I thought
He was really cute, too.

ROB, ELISABETH — And I remember um…um.
We all would like – went to the sauna…
And – and we like –

ROB — Heh!
See, all these stories like sound totally pervy!
But, you know it was –
Um.
A formative time….
As I said, but –

And I remember we all went to the sauna
And then we like –
All like –
Changed together.
And I remember like –
Thinking like:
"I really want to – have him see me change!" you know.
I really wanted him see me change!
Like out of my bathing suit, you know.

And – I don't think he…
(Oh no! I think he did!)
Yes! Now I remember. Okay, yes!

I remember he – he was watching me change.
And I knew that he was watching me change,

And I was like:
"Oh my god! YES!"
And uh. Heh!
Ha ha!

And that – so that was like – you know –
Kind of like –
Big Deal, for me.
And um. So – and that was probably
The last time I ever saw him,
But.

Act 3.0

ANNE

Oh! And also like – speaking of boys, too.
Um. One year –
I think this was in – eighth grade,
My parents – my father… had um.
This… um… business trip.
And it was up in New Hampshire.
And it was at this like really fancy like resort.
And I remember like at night
We would have these like banquets.
With like – the ice sculpture!
And it was like –
You know, my parents – had money,
But they weren't like rich,
You know, so.
But this was like all of the bosses, I guess –
And they all like – sponsored it.
So it was like all these like Rich People.
It was very exciting.
And everything was paid for and everything,

And. And…
We stayed in this condo…
With my father…
It was me and my father and –

(I don't think my mother – stayed in the condo.
She stayed in the hotel.)

And – and maybe my brother.
And then – um,

My father's friend,
Mr. Sherwood –
Who I really liked…
'Cause he was like a big drinker…
And he would always like –
Like tell all these like –
Raucus stories!

He was like a manly man!
And he had a helicopter.
(Um. Not a helicopter. A little small plane…)
And my father really liked him, you know.
My father didn't really
Have many friends, so, like –
He was like one of my father's friends,
And I like was kind of like –
Psyched!
That my father was friends with him.
'Cause he was like –
A really cool guy.
And anyway, Mr. Sherwood had –
(It was Don Sherwood…)

Um, he had a son.
And I don't remember his name,
But he was adopted. And um.

Oh – Peter!
Pete – Pete Jackson!

(Pete Jackson? Yes.)
Nonununo! So wait!
No! This was Mr. Jackson!
Yes.
(Don Sherwood's another guy.)

Mr. Jackson.
And he had a son,
Pete Jackson.
Annd uhm.
And he was very…
Like he was like –
This kid who seemed very like –
Heh!
I wanna say "disturbed"!

But he just seemed like –
I don't know.
Like kind of an angry kid.
But he was very cute.

And we would go swimming,
At the little place.
You know the – the little resort place.
Ahnd. Um.
Then we – we'd have
Like Movie Night, every night.

And we used to hold hands.
And.
And.
We –
Kissed!
One time.
And that was like –
“Oh my God.
That was my FIRST KISS!”

But – it wasn’t really like –
I don’t think we like –
You know.
Wasn’t like a French kiss or anything.
It was just like a normal
Kiss.
But I it felt like –
“Ohmygod!
This is my first real kiss!”
Sorta thing.

And I don’t really remember talking to him.
Heh!
At all.
I don’t think we ever like –
Really said anything beyond like –
One sentences.
Um. To one another, but –

But it –
You know it was like:
"Oh wow!
Like I have this sort of like lusty connection
With this kid, and I'll…
And I'll probably never see him again."

But that – I –
And that's probably why –
Like I felt like I could have this connection with him.
Like if he went to school with me
I probably would never have –
Been able to do that, you know.

But because like he would leave,
I just was like:
"Ohhh!"
You know,
So it was very exciting.
And um.

But my parents always like talked of –
Yeah.
I think he was –
Had like a –
Some sort of disorder.
Like Manic Depressive or something.

And so.
Actually, I've –

That's –
I think he's actually dead. Now.
I think he died.
And killed himself.
In his house or something.
But anyway.

Ummmm…
Soooho ho ho….

(big breath)

So Anyway! Um.
Let's see…
And then…

(sigh)

(I'm sure I'm skipping over stuff….)

JULIE

And then eighth grade.
I just became more and more – like
Awkward looking!
And my skin started to breakout.
And… I had braces…
And I just was like an awkward kid, you know.

And I was just
Kind of miserable.
And I would always just, you know.
Duck in the back.

Of class. And uh.
I had my few, like – girlfriends, but.

I – Junior High was very painful.
Heh he he heh.
It was like – heh!
"I'm getting this over right now!"

Act 3.1

ROB

Oh! And then –
The – did –
Did I – ?
Yeah. Eighth grade…
Oh! Eighth grade, too…
Um. My Parents!
At this time we bought a house in New Hampshire.
And so we would go up there.
Like once in a while,
And um. We went on a Ski Weekend,
And I brought Cheryl with me.

And. I remember… Uh…
Like my parents went out to dinner. Or som—
And like – they went to the store or something.
And – Cheryl was like:
"Let's go… let's go get some –"
No!
She brought some alcohol with her!
And I was like –

(gasp)

"How DARE you!"
And I got really mad at her, because um.
I felt like she was gonna get me in trouble.
You know, I was like:

"Fine if you wanna do that on your own time, Missy – but –"

I was like – I –
But – it was very strange how I got
Really mad at her.
Like I pulled this like moral authority trip
On her.
And um.
So, anyway.

ANNE

I think – at that time…
I did – Yeah.
We started –
(Was it in eighth grade? I think it was!)
So we –
We did start to drink. Um.
And I remember at the time, my sister – uhhh.

I think at this point
She was already… in college,
But – I had seen her like –
Getting drunk before, and I was like:
"Oh that's like –
That looks kinda cool." you know.
And um.

ROB

So, we used to –
My parents had this like huge liquor cabinet,
And – um.

That – it was like –
Liquor bottles that had been sitting there for years…
you know, Like every liquor imaginable!

Like mel— melon liquor, licorice liquor –
You know it was just –
Like weird…crappy stuff.
And we used to just take tiny bits of it.
And mix it all together.

And um – you know, just like sip.
Probably… you know,
By now – like a couple of shots –
And we'd get like – WASTED!
Heh! You know.

ALL — Wasted.

ROB — Right! Yeah!

ALL — Wasted!

ROB, JULIE, ANNE — Like off of – just off those two, um…
Sips of liquor or whatever.

ROB — So we started to do that for entertainment, too.
And we would bring it to like the movies.
We would bring it in hair –
Uh – hairspray bottles.
Um.

ALISON Oh! And yeah –
That's a whole other thing, too, like.

At that time, too,
In Junior High, like that's when you know
I started to like put hairspray in my hair…
And um I wore… makeup.
Annnd. Uh.

ALL And it – I –
Really – Had no idea what I
Was doing with all of that stuff.
But – um.
And I used to put hairspray like – right underneath my bangs.

So they'd stick up a little bit.
Like and kind of put it on the side a little bit, um.

ROB So yeah, we would go to the movies,
And put alcohol in like hairspray bottles.

(Exhale)

ALL Anyway. Um.
That's about that…!
And that's
THE
END!

Act 3.2

JULIE

No…!

Ha ha hah !
Haha!
Ummmm. Uhhhh. Yeah. Soooo.
Hold on one second.

What time is it?

Um.
Okay wait –
And then there's um.
Ninth grade…
A heh heh heh heh!

ALL

And ninth grade came along…
And this was high school, you know.

JULIE

Annnd Uhm.
Oh, you know I missed –
I skipped over some things!

I have to tell you about one thing
In junior high.
And this was in seventh grade.
Um.

And it was like my first – we –

You know we had dances, you know.
And um
The first dance –
That we went to…um.
It was like –
It was Fri –

ALL — It was a Friday night dance.

JULIE — And I think it was from… like "7 to 9!"
Maybe.
Or like maybe it was even –
No. I –
It was just probably

ALL — 7 to 9.
Annd. Um.

JULIE — You know, and it was in like the auditorium.
And they put like seats all around.
And – and then –
It was like dark.
And then –

They'd play songs, you know.
And… during the slow dances!
Um, you know everybody would dance with a boy!
And… I… so badly wanted to dance with Matt Wolf.
And um.
Matt Wolf,
Who sat in front of me in homeroom class.

And he was really ni—
Like he was nice to me, you know.
Like um – and I – I didn't think he liked me or anything, but –
I just thought we were like kind of like – you know.
On a good – basis with one another.

And so – I was g—
I was about to go up to ask him to dance.
And it was during um the song –
Orchestral Maneuvers in the Dark –
(sings) "Ne-neee-nee-neeh!"
Heh! How does it go?
Um. "If I left...

ALL Neh neh NEH... neh neh neh neh NEH neh neh..."

JULIE Anyways.
So I – loved that song, and it –
And it – and it was also that song...

ANNE Was it... *Sixteen*?

JULIE What?

ANNE It was a song that was in *Sixteen Candles*!
Um which was –
I watched that movie obsessively.
And um.
I wanted to be Molly Ringwald.
And – and she like –

Fell in love with –
This like beautiful hunk of a man…
In the – in the movie.

(Exhale)

So anyway!

JULIE

I – during that song I walked –
I was about to walk up to Matt Wolf…

And I was like just –
About to like tap him on his shoulder…
And then…

HE went and asked Jennifer Wilkes.
To go dance with him.
And I was like absolutely –
Like crushed.

So, I went to the bathroom,
And I was like crying.

And then my parents like picked me up.
And I was still crying.
And they're like
"What's wrong, Julie?"
And I was like "I don't wanna talk about it!"
Annnd, once again it was like at that – other time.
Where I like wanted my parents to be like:
"No! But tell us!"

You know. But they were like:
"Okay… She doesn't wanna talk about it, so."

Heh!
So I was just like – heh!
Sulking in the back.

Annnd. Um.
So. Yeeeah.
So anyway.
That was that.

Uhm.
But you know what?
Well, I think I have to go-oh!
And I think everyone's
Starting to leave.
I think I have to go!

ALL — Yeah.
Ohmygod!
You poor poor –
So sorry!

JULIE — Hehe he heh heh!

ALL — Ohhhh boy!
Okay.
Well um.

PRODUCTION CREDITS

Conceived and Directed by: PAVOL LISKA AND KELLY COPPER
From a telephone conversation with: KRISTIN WORRALL
Original music by: ROBERT M. JOHANSON and JULIE LAMENDOLA
Design by: PETER NIGRINI
Featuring: ELISABETH CONNER, ANNE GRIDLEY, ROBERT M. JOHANSON, JULIE LAMENDOLA, and ALISON WEISGALL
with ILAN BACHRACH, GABEL EIBEN, DANIEL GOWER, MATTHEW KORAHAIS, and KRISTIN WORRALL
Dramaturg: FLORIAN MALZACHER
Chorus director: NORA HERTLEIN
Production manager: DANY NAIERMAN
Audio engineer: DANIEL GOWER

A production of Nature Theater of Oklahoma and Burgtheater Wien in coproduction with Kampnagel Hamburg, le Festival d'Avignon, Théâtre de la Ville Paris, Kaaitheater Brussel, and Rosas.

Life and Times – Episode 2 was made possible with funding by the New England Foundation for the Arts' National Theater Pilot, with lead funding from the Andrew W. Mellon Foundation.

www.oktheater.org

ABOUT NATURE THEATER OF OKLAHOMA

"Personnel is being hired for the Theater in Oklahoma! The Great Nature Theater of Oklahoma is calling you! It's calling you today only! If you miss this opportunity, there will never be another! Anyone thinking of his future, your place is with us! All welcome! Anyone who wants to be an artist, step forward! We are the theater that has a place for everyone, everyone in his place! If you decide to join us, we congratulate you here and now! But hurry, be sure not to miss the midnight deadline! We shut down at midnight, never to reopen! Accursed be anyone who doesn't believe us!"

— Franz Kafka, *Amerika*

Nature Theater of Oklahoma is an OBIE-Award winning New York performance group under the direction of Pavol Liska and Kelly Copper. Since *Poetics: a ballet brut*, our first dance piece created as an ensemble, Nature Theater of Oklahoma has been devoted to making the work we don't know how to make, putting ourselves in impossible situations, and working from out of our own ignorance and unease. We strive to create an unsettling live situation that demands total presence from everyone in the room. We use the readymade material around us, found space, overheard speech, and observed gesture, and through extreme formal manipulation, and superhuman effort, we affect in our work a shift in the perception of everyday reality that extends beyond the site of performance and into the world in which we live.

Book design: Karinne Keithley Syers
Cover photograph: Nature Theater of Oklahoma
Printed on recycled paper.

53rd State Press publishes new writing for performance. It was founded in 2007 and is co-edited by Karinne Keithley Syers and Antje Oegel.

For more information or to order books, visit 53rdstatepress.org.
53rd State Press books are distributed to the trade by TCG/Consortium.

53SP 01 The Book of the Dog
53SP 02 Joyce Cho Plays
53SP 03 Nature Theater of Oklahoma's No Dice
53SP 04 Nature Theater of Oklahoma's Rambo Solo
53SP 05 When You Rise Up
53SP 06 Montgomery Park, or Opulence
53SP 07 Crime or Emergency
53SP 08 Off the Hozzle
53SP 09 A Map of Virtue and Black Cat Lost
53SP 10 Pig Iron: Three Plays
53SP 11 The Mayor of Baltimore and Anthem
53SP 12 Ich, KürbisGeist and The Secret Death of Puppets
53SP 13 Soulographie: Our Genocides
53SP 14 Nature Theater of Oklahoma's Life and Times: Episode 1
53SP 15 Nature Theater of Oklahoma's Life and Times: Episode 2
53SP 16 Nature Theater of Oklahoma's Life and Times: Episodes 3&4
53SP 17 The 53rd State Occasional No. 1